ABSTRACT

The Posse Comitatus Act (PCA) is often the so called linchpin that bars the use of our military forces to support and enforce civil law within the borders of the United States. This act has in effect, denied the citizens of the United States the utmost protection they should be afforded by the federal government by restricting the use of Department of Defense assets to be used as force multipliers to our federal law enforcement and intelligence agencies. The United States will be required to once again do more with less as federal spending is decreased on not only homeland defense, but its security as well.

The Federal Government will need to effectively utilize the combined resources of its numerous departments in order to accomplish this endeavor. Currently, the misinterpretation of the Posse Comitatus Act and the addition of subsequent restrictions have degraded our ability to properly protect the homeland. The Posse Comitatus Act is an ambiguous and highly misinterpreted law that needs to be rescinded and replaced with a new law that clearly identifies the terms in which the use of military forces in protecting the homeland is appropriate. This research paper focuses on the use of military forces in domestic affairs within the historical context of posse comitatus within the United States, the subsequent Posse Comitatus Act of 1878, the interpretation of the Posse Comitatus Act since its passage, and its current influence on the United States' ability to defend its homeland. This paper is a historical case study of the Posse Comitatus Act to include recommendations for how best to use our nation's military forces in a non-wartime environment in order to better ensure our nation's security in a whole of government approach.

ACKNOWLEDGEMENT

I would like to thank Joint Forces Staff College Associate Professor Glenn Jones for his support in writing this paper. His dedication and sheer interest in this endeavor has greatly enhanced its quality and personally has made the process of writing such a paper a much more enjoyable experience. I would also like to thank the Joint Forces Staff College for the opportunity to attend the Joint Advanced Warfighting School, granting me the privilege to be further educated amongst such a distinguished faculty and student body. I know this experience will provide me with the tools I will need to better my career and further the Department of Homeland Security in succeeding in its mission.

Lastly, I would like to thank my mother, Terry Schad and my sister, Vanessa Jenkin for their loving support during my time here at the Joint Forces Staff College. The Joint Advanced Warfighting School has been a truly challenging program for me and it has been due to their support that I have been able to find myself at its end successfully.

TABLE OF CONTENTS

INTRODUCTION

There have been few laws written that have caused as much controversy over the years as that of the Posse Comitatus Act. This law, enacted on 18 June 1878, consists of fifty-two words. Fifty-two words written into a single sentence that in comparison to language used in today's legal context, reads fairly simply. It is difficult to understand how a country that prides itself on being a nation ruled by law can consistently misinterpret fifty-two words. Seldom has so much been derived from so little written.[1]

> Whoever, except in cases and under circumstances expressly authorized by the Constitution or Act of Congress, willfully uses any part of the Army or the Air Force as a posse comitatus or otherwise to execute the laws shall be fined under this title or imprisoned not more than two years, or both.[2]

Title 18, U.S. Code, Section 1385 (1994)

In reading today's text of the Posse Comitatus Act, one needs to ask what the law says and doesn't say while understanding the pretext behind writing such a law. Over the past 133 years, the law has been used as a central reason why members of the U.S. military are unable to support and enforce civil law within the borders of the United States. "The Posse Comitatus Act has often been cited as a major constraint on the use of the military services to participate in homeland security, counterterrorism, civil disturbances, and similar domestic duties."[3] In effect, the law has denied the citizens of

---

[1] John R. Brinkerhoff, "The Posse Comitatus Act and Homeland Security," *HSI Journal of Homeland Security*, (February 2002): 1, http://www.homelandsecurity.org/journal/articles/brinkerhoffposseecomitatus.htm (accessed October 8, 2011).

[2] Cornell University Law School, "§ 1385. Use of Army and Air Force as Posse Comitatus," Legal Information Institute, http://www.law.cornell.edu/uscode/18/usc_sec_18_00001385----000-.html (accessed 30 October 2011).

[3] Brinkerhoff, "The Posse Comitatus Act and Homeland Security,", 1.

the United States the utmost protection they deserve from the federal government by restricting the use of Department of Defense assets as force multipliers to our federal law enforcement and intelligence agencies.

Since the events of September 11, 2001, the possibility of U.S. military assets called upon to participate in activities typically regarded as civil matters has increased significantly. With the primary objective of the Department of Defense being the defense of our Nation, it would seem that a law which predominantly denies the use of military assets to protect the homeland would be a direct impediment to the department in reaching its objective.[4] Due to the misinterpretation of the Posse Comitatus Act and further restrictions separating the Department of Defense from federal law enforcement, intelligence, and other civil authorities, the United States will be unable to accomplish this objective effectively and efficiently. To achieve this objective, the United States must bring all of her powers to bear.

As the United States prepares for deep spending cuts, it will need to make the most out of what limited resources it has at its disposal. The Federal Government will need to utilize the combined resources of its numerous departments in order to accomplish this endeavor effectively. The United States will remain incapable in securing areas presently exposed to significant risk unless it employs a whole of government approach. Currently, the misinterpretation of the Posse Comitatus Act and the addition of subsequent restrictions have degraded the United States' ability to protect the homeland properly. "Due to the combined effect of ignorance and careless diction, there is widespread misunderstanding of the principle terms used in connection with the

---

[4] U.S. Government. *The National Military Strategy of the United States of America*, 2011 (Washington, D.C.: Government Printing Office, February 2011) i.

enforcement of law by military means."[5] The Posse Comitatus Act is an ambiguous and highly misinterpreted law, which Congress needs to rescind and replace with a new law that clearly identifies the terms in which the use of military forces in protecting the homeland is appropriate. This research paper will illustrate the role our nation's military has played in domestic affairs both prior to and after the enactment of the Posse Comitatus Act. This paper will also identify where the Posse Comitatus Act has been misinterpreted and how this misinterpretation has negatively influence our Nation's ability to defend its homeland. This paper close by providing recommendations for how best to use our nation's military forces in a non-wartime environment in order to better ensure our nation's security in a whole of government approach.

---

[5] George S. Patton, Jr., "Federal Troops in Domestic Disturbances," *The Patton Society*, Patton Writings (November 1932): 1, http://www.pattonhq.com/textfiles/federal.html (accessed 9 October 2011).

CHAPTER 1:

UNDERSTANDING THE HISTORY BEHIND THE PCA

Posse Comitatus (Latin): Power of the county. The whole force of the county: that is, all the male members of a county over fifteen, who may be summoned by a sheriff to assist in preventing a riot, the rescue of prisoners, or other unlawful disorders.[1]

It is important to understand the history of posse comitatus before one asserts a position on the matter. Though the concept of posse comitatus can be traced back as far as 1181, it did not appear within English law until 1411.[2] It was not until the late eighteenth-century that the concept became a common practice amongst the population. "The American experience with posse comitatus began in the colonial period with the repeated use of military troops to suppress disorders in the colonies."[3] Britain increasingly used the practice of posse comitatus to assert its control over the colonies as colonial unrest grew. British military forces were widely dispatched throughout to act as a police force assuming the responsibility of civil authorities. In 1770, rioters in Boston were fired upon by the army, killing five men and wounding several others. The event would foreshadow the violent revolution to come and weigh heavily upon the minds that would forever shape a nation.

Soon after America had won her freedom from Britain, militias disbanded and citizen soldiers laid down their arms and began to return to their families. Many had

---

[1] E. Cobham Brewer, *Dictionary of Phrase and Fable* (Philadelphia: Henry Altemus Co., 1898), 2243.

[2] Stephen Young, "Features - The Posse Comitatus Act: A Resource Guide," *LLRX* (February 2003): 1, http://www.llrx.com/features/posse.htm (accessed 9 October 2011).

[3] Ibid.

been conscripted and fought with little to no compensation to help them pay for their living. Debt ran rampant and thousands lost everything, including their homes to confiscation. By 1786, the problem had reached critical mass when over 1000 armed farmers organized and marched on the city of Springfield, Massachusetts in order to halt the confiscations. Though the attack was defeated, it had threatened domestic tranquility throughout the states and convinced Congress that something needed to be done to strengthen the country's common resolve as well as protect the nation against all types of external and internal threats.[4]

> What stronger evidence can be given of the want of energy in our government than these disorders? If there exists not a power to check them, what security has a man for life, liberty, or property? Thirteen Sovereignties pulling against each other, and all tugging at the federal head will soon bring ruin to the whole. . .[5]
>
> George Washington

It was soon recognized that a minuteman army was unreliable, inefficient, and incapable of providing adequate security for the North American territories.[6] Following the Revolution, the founding fathers of the 1787 Constitutional Convention began to craft language directing the federal governmental powers to establish an army and a navy which could be used when called upon to execute the laws of the nation. Though the shadow of military force rising up against the very government they were to protect was

---

[4] Gregory J. W. Urwin, *The Army of the Constitution: The Historical Context* (Carlisle Barracks, PA: Strategic Studies Institute, U.S. Army War College, 2000) 36.

[5] Robert W. Coakley, *The Role of Federal Military Forces in Domestic Disorder 1789-1878* (Washington, DC: Center of Military History, 1988) 4-7.

[6] Richard H. Kohn, *Eagle and Sword* (New York: The Free Press, 1975) 9.

ever present in the minds of the framers of the Constitution, they chose not to regulate against it.[7]

On 21 June 1788, in order to establish justice, insure domestic tranquility, and provide for the common defense, the Constitution was ratified making the President of the United States the commander in chief of the military to include state militia and granting Congress control of its budget.[8]

> U.S. Constitution, Article II, Section 2:
>
> The President shall be Commander in Chief of the Army and Navy of the United States, and of the Militia of the several States, when called into the actual Service of the United States;[9]
>
> U.S. Constitution, Article I, Section 8:
>
> The Congress shall have power to raise and support Armies; to provide and maintain a Navy; to make Rules for the Government and Regulation of the land and naval Forces; to provide for calling forth the Militia to execute the Laws of the Union, suppress Insurrections and repel Invasions; to provide for organizing, arming, and disciplining, the Militia;[10]

Although the creation of a standing army and the control of such an army being given to the Federal government were debated by Federalist and anti-Federalist alike, the majority acknowledged that the newly formed nation was born in war and that its welfare could not be safeguarded without the ability to resort to force when required.

In 1789, during the first session of the First United States Congress and in accordance with Article III, section 1 of the Constitution, the federal judiciary system was established. In addition to the formation of the federal court system, the Judiciary

---

[7] Robert W. Coakley, The Role of Federal Military Forces in Domestic Disorder 1789-1878, 4-7.

[8] U.S. Government, "The Charters of Freedom," Archives, http://www.archives.gov/exhibits/charters/constitution.html (accessed 9 October 2011).

[9] Ibid.

[10] Ibid.

Act of 1789 created the Office of Attorney General as well as a United States Marshal position for each judicial district. Within Section 27 of the Act, the marshal was granted the "power to command all necessary assistance in the execution of his duty."[11] Though the act did not explicitly state that the marshal could use military forces in the performance of his duties, it would imply that using such force was permissible.

Though the American Revolutionary War had officially concluded in 1783, fighting continued over the control of territory east of the Mississippi River held by Native American nations. The western expansion of the United States under the concept of Manifest Destiny would lead to continuous conflict necessitating the use of the military to enforce federal law and maintain order. The so called "Indian Wars" were fought by settlers and the federal government alike with mounting losses as expansion grew.

In 1791, a U.S. Army force of approximately 1000 officers and men, led by General Arthur St. Clair, was engaged and decimated by an Indian force near the Wabash River on the Ohio-Indiana border. Within a few hours, approximately one-quarter of the entire U.S. Army had been wiped out. Primarily in response to the overwhelming U.S. losses at the Battle of the Wabash, the Second United States Congress in 1792 provided the President further authority to use military force, "whenever the laws of the United States shall be opposed or the execution thereof obstructed, in any state."[12] The President was authorized, "to call forth the militia of such state to suppress such combinations, and

---

[11] Constitution Society, "The Judiciary Act of 1789," http://www.constitution.org/uslaw/judiciary_1789.htm (accessed 15 October 2011).

[12] Constitution Society, "Miltia Act of 1792," http://www.constitution.org/mil/mil_act_1792.htm (accessed 15 October 2011).

to cause the laws to be duly executed."[13] The Act further provided for the organization of the state militias through conscription of "every able-bodied white male citizen...of the age of 18 years and under the age of 45... be enrolled in the militia."[14] The Militia Act of 1792 provided for the national defense by establishing a uniform militia throughout the United States.

In July 1794, in protest against an excise tax on domestically distilled spirits, farmers on the western frontier began to use violence and intimidation to prevent its collection. Small skirmishes broke out between protesters and militia while threats of looting, burning, and declaring independence from the United States began to grow.

> The laws of the United States are opposed, and the execution therefore obstructed by combinations too powerful to be suppressed by the ordinary course of Judicial proceedings or by the powers vested in the Marshal of the district.[15]

> Associate Supreme Court Justice James Wilson

Confronted with an armed insurrection, President Washington sent commissioners to meet with the leaders of the protest in order to negotiate peaceful terms while sending out orders to raise a militia army in the event negotiations failed. The commissioners were able to narrowly pass a resolution with protesters agreeing to renounce violence and submit to U.S. laws. The resolution however, was not accepted by many and opposition remained widespread compelling the commissioners to recommend the use of the military to enforce the laws. The insurrection collapsed before a federalized militia force of approximately 13,000 men could arrive. Though violent opposition had ended, the militia occupied the area, pursuing and arresting those involved in leading the rebellion.

---

[13] Ibid.

[14] Ibid.

[15] Leland D. Baldwin, *Whiskey Rebels: The Story of a Frontier Uprising* (Pittsburgh: The University of Pittsburgh Press, 1939), 184–185.

Over the next several years, both regular and militia forces would be called upon to uphold the laws of the nation. In many cases, the need for efficiency coupled with the need for expediency of action, compelled the federal government to increase its reliance on employing the regular army.[16] In 1807, at the request of President Thomas Jefferson, Congress granted the President the authority to employ both land and naval forces to uphold the laws of the nation.

> [I]n all cases of insurrection, or obstruction to the laws, either of the United States, or of any individual state or territory, where it is lawful for the President of the United States to call forth the militia for the purpose of suppressing such insurrection, or of causing the laws to be duly executed, it shall be lawful for him to employ, for the same purposes, such part of the land or naval force of the United States, as shall be judged necessary, having first observed all the pre-requisites of the law in that respect.[17]

Insurrection Act of 1807

Prior to this act, though regular military forces had already been used to enforce the laws of the nation, no such law existed to regulate its practice. This act significantly strengthened the President's position to authorize the use of regular military forces in cases of civil unrest. Now, the federal government could use not only state militias to enforce the laws of the United States, but it could also use the full weight of the US Army and Navy.

In 1850, in recognition of Southern support for California's admission into the Union as a free state and ending the slave trade in the District of Columbia, Congress enacted the Fugitive Slave Act. The act declared that all runaway slaves be returned to their owners and made United States Marshals primarily responsible for the enforcement

---

[16] Robert W. Coakley, The Role of Federal Military Forces in Domestic Disorder 1789-1878, 69-77.

[17] San Diego State University, "Insurrection Act, 1807," ROHAN, http://www-rohan.sdsu.edu/dept/polsciwb/brianl/docs/1807InsurrectionAct.pdf (accessed 16 October 2011).

of the act. The marshals, having granted to them the "power to command all necessary assistance in the execution of his duty" by the Judiciary Act of 1789, were further granted under the Fugitive Slave Act the authority to compel citizens to assist the marshal in the course of performing his duties.

> To summon and call to their aid the bystanders, or **posse comitatus** of the proper county, when necessary to ensure a faithful observance of the clause of the Constitution referred to, in conformity with the provisions of this act; and all good citizens are hereby commanded to aid and assist in the prompt and efficient execution of this law, whenever their services may be required.[18]
>
> Fugitive Slave Act of 1850

The act, signed into law by President Fillmore, paved the way for law enforcement officials to utilize the military in enforcing federal law. The Fugitive Slave Act would bring significant opposition from northern free-states where both militia and regular forces would be called upon in numerous instances to sustain law. As the use of the military to support the enforcement of law became more prevalent, debate began to arise over whether the military could be included within a marshal's posse comitatus. Initial findings from the Senate Judiciary Committee confirmed a marshal's authority to call upon both the militia or regular forces when required.[19]

> The committee is not aware of any reason that exempts the citizens who constitute the military and naval forces of the United States from like liability to duty. Because men are soldiers or sailors, they cease not to be citizens; and while acting under the call and direction of the civil authority, they may act with more efficiency, and without objection, in an organized form, under appropriate subordinate command.[20]
>
> Senate Judiciary Committee, 1851

---

[18] The National Center for Public Policy Research, "Fugitive Slave Act 1850," http://www.nationalcenter.org/FugitiveSlaveAct.html (accessed 16 October 2011).

[19] Robert W. Coakley, The Role of Federal Military Forces in Domestic Disorder 1789-1878, 129-131.

[20] Ibid., 130.

By 1854, the increased use of the military by marshals to enforce the Fugitive Slave Act further incited controversy over the legitimacy of the practice. In 1854, in an attempt to galvanize the federal government's authority in this matter and improve the enforcement of the Fugitive Slave Act, Caleb Cushing, attorney general for President Franklin Pierce, issued a legal opinion which clearly defined the authority of US marshals in constituting a posse comitatus.

> A marshal of the United States, when opposed in the execution of his duty by unlawful combinations, has authority to summon the entire able-bodied force of his precinct as a posse comitatus. This authority comprehends, not only bystanders and other citizens generally, but any and all organized armed force, whether militia of the State, or officers, soldiers, sailors, and marines of the United States.[21]
>
> Attorney General Caleb Cushing, 27 May 1854

What was to become known as the Cushing Doctrine, widely encouraged the use of the military as a law enforcement body. The use of the military within a posse comitatus became prominent within the western frontier, where they were the only armed force available to assist in the enforcement of the law.

With growing unrest over the issue of slavery between northern free-states and southern slave-states, political tension began to escalate and civil disobedience began to turn violent. In 1859, revolutionary abolitionist leader John Brown supported by 18 men attacked and seized the federal armory at Harpers Ferry. Brown had hoped to seize the weapons cache and use it to arm local slaves. Local militia soon surrounded the armory and cut off any chance of escape for Brown and his men. Under the orders of President James Buchanan, Colonel Robert E. Lee was to lead a detachment of U.S. Marines and march on Harpers Ferry, secure the facility, and arrest those responsible.

---

[21] Robert W. Coakley, The Role of Federal Military Forces in Domestic Disorder 1789-1878, 132.

Soon after the arrival of Lee and his men, Brown and those who survived the ensuing gun battle were captured and charged with the crimes of murder, conspiracy, and treason against the Commonwealth of Virginia. Upon being found guilty of all three counts, Brown, noting the inevitability of a war to come, exclaimed: "I, John Brown, am now quite certain that the crimes of this guilty land will never be purged away, but with blood. I had, as I now think, vainly flattered myself that without very much bloodshed it might be done"[22].

The American Civil War had begun with the attack on Fort Sumter by Confederate forces in April of 1861. Three months later, Congress responded by vastly strengthening the President's authority to use both the militia and regular forces to suppress insurrections and execute the laws of the Union.[23]

> That whenever, by reason of unlawful obstructions, combinations or assemblages of persons, or rebellion against the authority of the government of the United States, it shall become impracticable, in the judgment of the President ... to enforce, by the ordinary course of judicial proceedings, the laws of the United States within any state or territory ... it shall be lawful for the President ... to call forth the militia of any or all of the states of the Union, and to employ such part of the land and naval forces of the United States as he may deem necessary to enforce the faithful execution of the laws ... or to suppress such rebellion in whatever state or territory thereof the laws ... may be forcibly opposed or the execution thereof forcibly obstructed.[24]

Suppression of the Rebellion Act of 1861

In August of 1861, President Lincoln proclaimed that the inhabitants of the seceded states were "in a state of insurrection against the United States" which sanctioned his use of the military to suppress the rebellion. This law would remain a

---

[22] West Virginia Division of Culture and History, "John Brown and the Harpers Ferry Raid," West Virginia Archives and History, http://www.wvculture.org/history/jnobrown.html (accessed 29 October 2011).

[23] Robert W. Coakley, The Role of Federal Military Forces in Domestic Disorder 1789-1878, 228.

[24] Ibid.

permanent statutory authority to be used by presidents as the predominant basis for military intervention in domestic disorders.[25]

As the country's attention became fixated on civil war, concerns over the use of the military to enforce civil law began to recede into the shadows. It would not be until after America's Civil War that the practice of posse comitatus would return to the forefront in its use to bring fundamental social, economic, and political change to the nation.

The use of the military in civil governmental affairs would not be more apparent than during the period of Reconstruction. With the assassination of President Abraham Lincoln and the Confederacy's surrender ending America's Civil War, President Andrew Johnson would need to leverage the whole weight of the federal government to repair a severely fractured nation. In an effort to reestablish the rule of law by the federal government, Southern states were appointed provisional military governors. During this period, the military administered local government and exercised police and judicial functions.

Johnson focused much of his efforts on the repatriation of the southern states back into the Union and less so on what to do about the newly freed black population. The resurgence of conservative state governments across the South, permitted by Johnson's liberal approach to Reconstruction, allowed for unimpeded racism against the black populace. The establishment of "Black Codes" by pro-Confederate parties soon swept throughout southern states aiming to severely restrict the rights of blacks. The institution of "Black Codes" outraged northern opinion and in 1866, Congress passed the Civil

---

[25] Ibid., 228-9.

Rights Act granting citizenship to anyone born within the United States (excluding

Native Americans). The Act was directed at providing freed slaves with a range of civil

rights that were enjoyed by white citizens.[26]

> All persons within the jurisdiction of the United States shall have the same right in every State and Territory to make and enforce contracts, to sue, be parties, give evidence, and to the full and equal benefit of all laws and proceedings for the security of persons and property as is enjoyed by white citizens, and shall be subject to like punishment, pains, penalties, taxes, licenses, and exactions of every kind, and to no other.[27]
>
> Civil Rights Act of 1866

The enforcement of the Civil Rights Act of 1866 was left to the federal marshals

who were empowered with the authority, "to summon and call to their aid the bystanders

or posse comitatus of the proper county, or such portion of the land or naval forces of the

United States, or of the militia, as may be necessary to the performance of the duty with

which they are charged,"[28] as identified within the Act.

Three short months after the passage of the Civil Rights Act, the 14th Amendment

to the United States Constitution was proposed, declaring all people born in the United

States or who naturalized to be citizens and that "no state shall make or enforce any law

which shall abridge the privileges or immunities of citizens of the United States; nor shall

any State deprive any person of life, liberty, or property, without due process of law; nor

deny to any person within its jurisdiction the equal protection of the laws."[29] The 14th

Amendment was to provide the firm Constitutional foundation for enacting the 1866

---

[26] PBS, "1866 Civil Rights Act," PBS Online, http://www.pbs.org/wgbh/amex/reconstruction/activism/ps_1866.html (accessed 30 October 2011).

[27] Ibid.

[28] Ibid.

[29] Steve Mount, "US Constitution – Admendment 14," US Constitution Online, http://www.usconstitution.net/xconst_Am14.html (accessed 6 November 2011).

Civil Rights Act and assure citizenship and equal protection under the law. The amendment would also deem any laws previously enacted, such as the "Black Codes", unconstitutional.

With the enactment of the Civil Rights Act and the proposal of the 14th Amendment, dissention began to grow amongst southern states. White majorities, opposing the new laws and aiming to restore white rule, began to organize utilizing intimidation and violence against blacks and their supporters. Most of these groups were made up of veterans of the Confederate Army and wielded substantial influence both socially and politically within the southern states.

With southern state legislatures refusing to ratify the 14th Amendment, Congress enacted Reconstruction Acts beginning in 1867. Within these acts, Congress declared that "no legal State governments or adequate protection for life or property," existed within the southern states not already readmitted to the Union. Until each state established a congressionally approved state constitution and ratified the 14th Amendment, they would be divided into five military districts under the command of a military officer selected by the President of the United States. State authority was considered to be null and void and the military commander, provided with sufficient military force, was assigned to enforce all civil laws and pass judgment upon those who violated such laws. In the years to come, southern states would rely upon Federal military forces to protect civil rights and squelch violence.

By 1868, seven of the eleven southern states, having ratified the 14th Amendment and established an approved state constitution, had been readmitted to the Union and were allowed once again to self-govern, though many of the newly formed state governments still required military assistance from the federal government in order to enforce the new laws. Under the direction of Attorney General William Evarts, in citing the 1854 Cushing Doctrine, states could acquire support under the authority of the federal marshal who was empowered to call upon the military to assist as necessary in the performance of his assigned duties. The War Department in turn clarified Evarts' opinion by ensuring the sanctity of the military chain of command and directed that all requests for military support, in cases where there was no emergent need, be forwarded to the President for approval. Evarts' opinion therefore, led to innumerable requests by US marshals and county sheriffs, both in the South and the West, for troop assistance in the enforcement of law.[30]

By 1870, all southern states were readmitted to the Union having complied with the terms set forth by the Reconstruction Acts. Military governance was therefore relinquished and southern states now loyal to the Union were once again under civil rule. "Never before or after, within the continental boundaries of the United States, did [the military] exercise police and judicial functions, oversee local governments, or deal with domestic violence on the scale it did," than during the period of Reconstruction.[31] Though the authority to self-govern was once again in the hands of the individual states, military forces would remain to assist the newly formed state governments in the execution of their responsibilities until 1877.

With governance authority returned to the southern states, groups such as the Ku Klux Klan gained significant influence over positions of political power. The Klan soon

---

[30] Robert W. Coakley, The Role of Federal Military Forces in Domestic Disorder 1789-1878, 300.

[31] Ibid., 268.

spread into nearly every southern state providing an armed force to those that desired the restoration of white supremacy. Though the Klan's focus was to suppress the black population, it took aim at Republicans who the Klan believed to be at the center of the rising black movement. The Klan responded with violence by assassinating political leaders, committing mass murders, inciting riots, and destroying property.[32]

Between 1870 and 1871, Congress would pass a series of acts aimed at enforcing the provisions of the 14th and 15th Amendments. Known as the Enforcement Acts and Ku Klux Klan Act, these acts further authorized the military to suppress the Klan in support of southern Republican governments. Under the direction of the federal marshal, the military conducted massive arrests and trials imposing some 3,000 indictments throughout the southern states. The acts and the Cushing Doctrine had enabled the federal government to suppress the violence conducted by the Klan and southern support for the reinstatement of white rule began to shift to more democratic means.[33]

Over the next several years, though the use of the military to enforce civil law remained a fairly common practice, the number of engagements in which they would be involved began to decrease considerably. Units were routinely used to safeguard election polls, provide for the preservation of the peace at political events, and further support civil authorities in enforcing federal laws. The role of the military in enforcing the laws of the nation though would weigh heavily on the minds of many southerners for years to come.[34]

---

[32] Ibid., 299-307.

[33] Eric Foner, Reconstruction: America's Unfinished Revolution, 1863–1877 (New York: Harper & Row, 1988) 457.

[34] Robert W. Coakley, The Role of Federal Military Forces in Domestic Disorder 1789-1878, 334-341.

With the inauguration of Rutherford B. Hayes as the 19th President of the United States, the period of Reconstruction officially ended in 1877. The withdrawal of federal troops throughout the southern states began almost immediately. The newly controlled Democratic Congress took aim at limiting what they believed to be the misuse of the military under the Cushing Doctrine in meddling in state affairs. In May of 1878, Representative J. Proctor Knott of Kentucky introduced what was to become the Posse Comitatus Act.[35]

---

[35] Brinkerhoff, "The Posse Comitatus Act and Homeland Security,", 3.

CHAPTER 2:

UNDERSTANDING THE PCA AS IT WAS WRITTEN

> From and after the passage of this act it shall not be lawful to employ any part of the Army of the United States as a posse comitatus, or otherwise, for the purpose of executing the laws, except in such cases and under such circumstances as such employment of said force may be expressly authorized by the Constitution or by act of Congress; no money appropriated by this act shall be used to pay any of the expenses incurred in the employment of any troops in violation of this section and any person willfully violating the provisions of this section shall be deemed guilty of a misdemeanor, and on conviction thereof shall be punished by fine not exceeding ten thousand dollars or imprisonment not exceeding two years, or by both such fine and imprisonment.[1]

Section 15, chapter 263, Acts of the 2nd session of the 45th Congress, 1878

Knott's amendment, having passed both the House and Senate, was signed into law by President Hayes on 18 June 1878. Many believed that the passing of the act was a direct result of the use of federal military forces during the period of Reconstruction. The act was championed by southern democrats striving for the reestablishment of white rule believing the act would significantly reduce the government's ability to enforce federal laws within the individual states.

Since the time the United States declared its independence, the military served as the only capable law enforcement body available to the federal government in ensuring its authority was respected and its laws were carried out.[2] Some believed the act diminished the President's power to use the military to repress internal disorder. Others believed its intent was to limit the use of the military by local governments and law

---

[1] Robert W. Coakley, The Role of Federal Military Forces in Domestic Disorder 1789-1878, 344.

[2] Clayton D. Laurie and Ronald H. Cole, *The Role of Federal Military Forces in Domestic Disorder 1877-1945* (Washington, DC: Center of Military History, 1997) vii.

enforcement entities without the consent of the federal government. Since the act's passage, it has been at the center of much debate as to its true meaning.

Though amended in 1956 to include the United States Air Force, and again in 1959 to make it applicable to the state of Alaska, and lastly in 1994 to remove the upper limit to the attached fine, the language of the Posse Comitatus Act has remained essentially intact. So why is it that the Posse Comitatus Act is so widely misunderstood?

> Whoever, except in cases and under circumstances expressly authorized by the Constitution or Act of Congress, willfully uses any part of the Army or the Air Force as a posse comitatus or otherwise to execute the laws shall be fined under this title or imprisoned not more than two years, or both.[3]

Title 18, U.S. Code, Section 1385

In reading the above act, it only applies to the Army and the Air Force. It says nothing about the Navy or the Marine Corps, though the Department of Defense has consistently held that both services should perform in accordance with the law. The act does not apply to the Coast Guard or the National Guards of the individual states. Even when the National Guards are federalized, there is no provision within the act restricting their use. The act does not prevent the use of *any* of the services in supporting or executing the laws of the United States if authorized by the President. The act also identifies those who would be in violation of the law as being neither the Army nor the Air Force, but rather the body that employs them. This could be why no one has ever been prosecuted under this law.

The President's authority to use military forces in enforcing civil law remained intact under the Posse Comitatus Act, but the utilization of such force could not be used

---

[3] Cornell University Law School, "§ 1385. Use of Army and Air Force as Posse Comitatus,".

on any lesser authority than that of the President.[4] All the act really did was to rescind the authorities of the federal marshal to utilize the armed forces of the United States as a posse comitatus based solely upon the marshal's discretion.

Legislative and executive action in the years prior to the enactment of the Posse Comitatus Act confirmed that the use of the military to preserve domestic order, either as part of a posse comitatus or otherwise, was an accepted feature of American life under the Constitution. The Posse Comitatus Act was aimed at reversing this feature and not at denying the President's ability to use federal troops to enforce law. In the act, the President retained the authority under federal law to use the military in executing the laws of the United States; however it overturned the long-standing practice articulated by Attorney General Cushing in 1854.

> A marshal of the United States, when opposed in the execution of his duty by unlawful combinations, has authority to summon the entire able-bodied force of his precinct as a posse comitatus. This authority comprehends, not only bystanders and other citizens generally, but any and all organized armed force, whether militia of the State, or officers, soldiers, sailors, and marines of the United States.[5]
>
> Attorney General Caleb Cushing, 27 May 1854

The Cushing Doctrine's practice was initially used to support federal marshals in their enforcement of the Fugitive Slave Act within the Northern states and was hailed by Southern slaveholding states as being necessary to execute such a law. Southern support for the doctrine substantially diminished during the Civil War and Reconstruction periods when marshals, supported by military forces, were directed to enforce civil rights laws and protect the newly freed black population.

---

[4] Robert W. Coakley, The Role of Federal Military Forces in Domestic Disorder 1789-1878, 344.

[5] Ibid., 132.

In trying to understand the "true" congressional intent of the Posse Comitatus Act, Representative Knott himself stated that the act was "designed to put a stop to the practice, which had become fearfully common of military officers of every grade answering the call of every marshal and deputy marshal to aid in the enforcement of the laws."[6]

President Hayes, having signed the bill into law, concurred that the act limited the marshal's authority to use the military, but he did not believe that the law applied to presidential authority. A few months after the bill's passage, President Hayes deployed troops in a seventeen-month military intervention to enforce judicial process and enforce the law within the state of New Mexico.[7]

President Chester Arthur, being confronted with similar lawlessness in Arizona between the years of 1881 and 1882, requested Congress's interpretation of the act due to what he believed to be ambiguity of presidential power within its language. The Senate Judiciary Committee replied by identifying that the act was directed at restricting a federal marshal's authority to call into service military members during the execution of the law and not at limiting the authority of the President.

> The posse comitatus clause referred to arose out of an implied authority to the marshals and their subordinates executing the laws to call upon the Army just as they would upon bystanders who, if the Army responded, would have command of the Army or so much of it as they had, just as they would of the bystanders, and would direct them what to do.
>
> In all these cases, the President of the United States having the power of employing any part of the Army ... to assist in the execution of the laws ... retains the dominion over

---

[6] Gary Felicetti and John Luce, "The Posse Comitatus Act: Setting the Record Straight on 124 Years of Mischief and Misunderstanding Before Any More Damage is Done." *Miltary Law Review* Vol 175, Rev. 86 (March 2003): 118, https://www.hsdl.org/?view&did=439130 (accessed 19 November 2011).

[7] Ibid., 119.

this Army himself and the soldiers under command of their own officers to aid the civil authority, instead of being under the command of the marshal ....[8]

13 CONG. REC. 3458 (1882)

"Whoever, except in cases and under circumstances expressly authorized by the Constitution or Act of Congress..."[9] Under the Constitution, the President, charged with the faithful execution of the laws of the United States, "shall be Commander in Chief of the Army and Navy of the United States, and of the Militia of the several States, when called into the actual Service of the United States."[10] The Constitution contains no explicit limits on the President's use of the armed forces to carry out the executive function beyond those contained in the Bill of Rights.[11]

The failure to prohibit military participation in civil affairs suggests that Representative Knott and the remaining framers of the Posse Comitatus Act never intended to restrict the federal government's use of the military, but rather believed the Cushing Doctrine undermined the system of checks and balances that was emplaced to prevent its abuse. The arguments by those who cite the nineteenth century remnant as banning the armed forces from participating in civil affairs are not supported by the act's historical record or its text.

It is apparent that the eighteenth century environment in which the Constitution was written was vastly different than that of the environment in which we live today. At the time of it's drafting, many feared the threat of a standing national army which could

---

[8] Ibid., 121.

[9] Cornell University Law School, "§ 1385. Use of Army and Air Force as Posse Comitatus,".

[10] U.S. Government, "The Charters of Freedom,".

[11] Gary Felicetti and John Luce, "The Posse Comitatus Act: Setting the Record Straight on 124 Years of Mischief and Misunderstanding Before Any More Damage is Done.", 94.

rise and crush the young republic's newly acquired independence. Having endured

British oppression, the threat of tyranny by a strong federal government and its ability to

use force by military means was on the minds of many forefathers during our

government's conception. As the United States' political culture has matured over the

last two centuries, its fear of a tyrannical central government and its use of military force

to suppress the masses have significantly faded. The use of military force in domestic

operations has exceeded well over two-hundred occasions since America's adoption of its

Constitution.[12] Today, the United States military is part of our national identity and has

been instrumental in protecting this country's independence against threats both foreign

and domestic.

There has been an inherent aversion by Americans in using military service

members as a policing body. At present, we have large national law enforcement

agencies whose members bear little distinction between military soldier and police

officer. The use of the military to execute the laws of the United States is a widely

unpopular vision yet the majority of Americans accept an ever increasing presence of

federal, state, and local law enforcement.

The Department of Defense and the individual military services have also been

cited as a supportive source in the erroneous application of the Posse Comitatus Act as

they themselves do not wish to become involved in civil affairs.[13] Much of this

conviction stems from the military's belief that its service members are inadequately

trained to deal with civil affairs and their fear of the increased scrutiny inherent in dealing

with operations oriented domestically versus those abroad. In response, the Department

---

[12] Brinkerhoff, "The Posse Comitatus Act and Homeland Security,", 5.

[13] Ibid., 6.

has created a significant body of policy and regulation extralegally in the form of directives and military service regulations pertaining to its ability to engage in civil affairs.[14] Though there is much truth in these views, they remain an anticatalyst in using military means within the borders of the United States to execute its laws.

Case law and judicial opinions have also had a significant hand in the Posse Comitatus Act's interpretation or in the preponderance of the cases, its misinterpretation. As many have looked to the Posse Comitatus Act to provide guidance as to the employment of military forces in civil affairs, much has been read into the ambiguous law. These attempts to clarify the law, most based on a presumption significantly at variance with the law itself, have only added to its confusion and resulted in departing further from the law's original intent.[15]

---

[14] Brinkerhoff, "The Posse Comitatus Act and Homeland Security,", 6.
[15] Ibid.

CHAPTER 3:

THE PCA AND BEYOND

The Act clearly did not end the practice of using military forces in civil affairs. Since the Posse Comitatus Act's inception in 1878, the military has been used in numerous cases to enforce both federal and state laws mainly aimed at quelling disorders and instituting desegregation. In the decades that followed the enactment of the Posse Comitatus Act, the United States underwent fundamental change through modernization. Unlike the earlier role the military played in domestic affairs, which arose largely from the political issues of nation building and concerns over the extent and power of federal authority, the post-Reconstruction use of the military involved primarily industrial disputes and social and racial tensions.[1]

During this period, the military would be required to engage on a national scene highly influenced by a large influx of immigrants from ethnic groups and world regions previously unrepresented in American society; the organization of labor unions, some radical in action and thought; and the shift of economic and political power from local to national levels amid rapid and uncontrolled industrialization and urbanization.[2] Although its primary mission was to defend the nation's borders against foreign enemies and to protect the rapidly expanding western frontier, the military remained the only capable body available to the federal government to maintain internal civil order.[3]

---

[1] Clayton D. Laurie and Ronald H. Cole, The Role of Federal Military Forces in Domestic Disorder 1877-1945, 3.

[2] Ibid.

[3] Ibid., 4.

The effects of the Posse Comitatus Act were most prominent within the western territories where marshals relied heavily upon their authority to utilize federal military forces under the Cushing Doctrine to assist in carrying out their duties. The enforcement of law was the responsibility of territorial governments that lacked the proper resources to confront the vast lawlessness that existed in the Trans-Mississippi west. The Posse Comitatus Act required state and territorial governors who wanted military assistance to request such assistance from the President. This process was complex and time consuming often leading to the military being incapable of providing timely and needed assistance. Federal and local law enforcement officials were too few in numbers to deal with the ever increasing outbreaks of organized violence that existed in the expansive, sparsely populated West.

> In the new and sparsely populated regions of the West, to say to robbers and thieves that they shall not be taken on writ unless the sheriff and his local posse is able to capture them without the aid from soldiers, is almost to grant them immunity from arrest. In these regions the Army is the power chiefly relied upon by the law-abiding people for protection.[4]

> Secretary of War George W. McCrary, 1878

In addition to dealing with widespread violence emanating throughout the West from various range wars, bands of outlaws and hostile Indians, the military would be required to intervene in instances of civil unrest stemming from racial tensions. In the territories of Wyoming and Washington, the military was used to quell violence between white and Chinese miners between the years of 1885 and 1886. The military was used to preserve the peace, provide security to life and property, and prevent obstruction to local authorities in their enforcement of the laws.

---

[4] Clayton D. Laurie and Ronald H. Cole, The Role of Federal Military Forces in Domestic Disorder 1877-1945, 57.

With the Posse Comitatus Act firmly in place, the military was instructed to only assume law enforcement authority if civil powers were prevented in carrying out their duties by opposition resorting to acts of violence. The use of military force in domestic matters under the Posse Comitatus Act would be subject to explicit instructions drafted by the executive branch, approved by the President, and limited to the specific event in which the federal government intervened. No longer was the military commander able to provide unrestricted assistance to civil authorities as he was authorized prior to the enactment of the Posse Comitatus Act. The anti-Chinese riots in Wyoming and Washington territories had caught the residing administration by surprise and demonstrated government confusion about the objectives of military intervention and how to bring such intervention about under the onus of the Posse Comitatus Act.[5]

Over the next several years, the intervention by the federal government in which it warranted the use of federal military force in civil affairs declined as both state and federal civil officials began to rely greater upon private security, local police, and State National Guard forces to quell civil disorder.[6] By 1894, nationwide social and labor unrest would compel the federal government to once again use military forces in various locations throughout the United States and its territories to restore order and protect property. In a period spurred by twenty percent unemployment rates, large bands of the unemployed and disconnected protested by interrupting rail service, affecting nearly 41,000 miles of track in twenty-seven states, much of which was in federal receivership.[7]

---

[5] Jerry M. Cooper, The Army and civil disorder: Federal military intervention in labor disputes, 1877-1900 (Westport: Greenwood Press, 1980), 86-87.

[6] Clayton D. Laurie and Ronald H. Cole, The Role of Federal Military Forces in Domestic Disorder 1877-1945, 111.

[7] Ibid., 125.

The difficulties presented by the Posse Comitatus Act were met through the use of presidential directives citing anti-insurrection laws RS 5297 and RS 5298.

> R.S.5297 provides: In case of insurrection in any State against the government thereof, it shall be lawful for the President, on the application of the legislature of such State, or of the Executive, when the legislature cannot be convened, to call forth such number of the militia of any other state or states as he deems sufficient to suppress such insurrection, or such part of the land and naval forces of the United States as he deems necessary.[8]

> R.S.5298 provides: Whenever by reason of unlawful obstructions, combinations or assemblages of persons, or rebellion against the authority of the United States, it shall become impracticable, in the judgment of the President, to enforce, by the ordinary laws of judicial procedure, the laws of the United States within any State or Territory, it shall be lawful for the President to employ such part of the land and naval forces of the United States as he may deem necessary to enforce the lawful execution of the laws of the United States .[9]

The military's response varied from region to region; in the Midwest the military worked with State National Guardsmen, marshals, and city police to restore order; while in the West, the military served as the dominant law enforcement body as no other capable organization existed.[10]

In an effort to further comply with the restrictions set by the Posse Comitatus Act, the Commanding General of the Army, John M. Schofield, developed specific military doctrine to address military chain of command issues while participating in civil disturbances.

> The troops are employed as a part of a military power of the United States, and act under the orders of the President ... and his military subordinates. They cannot be directed to act under the orders of any civil officer. The commanding officers of the troops so employed are directly responsible to their military supervisors. Any unlawful or unauthorized act on their part would not be excusable on the ground of any order or request received by them from a marshal or any other civil officer.[11]

General Order 15, Paragraph 490, Article 52

---

[8] George S. Patton, Jr., "Federal Troops in Domestic Disturbances,", 1.

[9] Ibid.

[10] U.S. War Department, *Annual Report of the Secretary of War, 1894* (Washington, DC: Government Printing Office, 1895) 4, 11, 57-8.

[11] Ibid., 57-9.

General Order 15 became the Army's first attempt to establish doctrine regulating the military's role during a federal response to such disturbances. It was aimed at making sure the military continued to operate free from the control of competing parties and that its intervention to restore order remained impartial. As General Order 15 addressed organizational issues when employed in domestic affairs, the question then turned to how the military should operate during its intervention. In July of 1894, Schofield issued General Order 23 which became the foundation for Army civil disturbance doctrine and provided general operating guidelines for military personnel in such disturbances.

> Troops called into action against a mob forcibly resisting or obstructing the execution of the laws of the United States or attempting to destroy property belonging to, or under the protection of, the United States are governed by the general regulations of the Army and apply military tactics in respect to the manner in which they shall act to accomplish the desired end.
>
> It is a purely tactical question in what manner they shall use the weapons with which they are armed; whether by fire of musketry and artillery, or by the use of the bayonet and saber, or by both, and at what stage of the operations each or either mode of attack shall be employed. This tactical question shall be decided by the immediate commander of the troops, according to his judgment of the situation.
>
> The fire of troops should be withheld until timely warning has been given to the innocent who may be mingled with the mob. Troops must never fire into a crowd unless ordered by their commanding officer, except that single selected sharp shooters may shoot down individual rioters who have fired upon or thrown missiles at the troops.
>
> As a general rule, only the bayonet (or saber) should be used against mixed crowds in the first stages of a revolt, but as soon as sufficient warning has been given to enable the innocent to separate themselves from the guilty, the action of the troops should be governed solely by the tactical considerations involved in the duty they are ordered to perform. They should make their flow so effective as to promptly suppress all resistance to lawful authority, and should stop the destruction of life the moment lawless resistance has ceased. Punishment belongs not to the troops, but to the courts of justice.[12]
>
> Section III, Paragraph 8, A.R. 50050

---

[12] George S. Patton, Jr., "Federal Troops in Domestic Disturbances,", 1.

By August of 1894, the combined efforts of federal, state, and local intervention had successfully ended the countywide turmoil caused by the mass of social and labor unrest. Military commanders successfully coordinated operations avoiding violations of the Posse Comitatus Act while maintaining compliance with General Orders 15 and 23.

In May of 1895, the U.S. Supreme Court, addressing a petition by convicted American Railway Union President Eugene Debs, ruled that "the strong arm of the National Government may brush aside all obstructions to the freedom of interstate commerce or the transportation of the mails. If the emergency arises, the Army of the nation and all its militias, are at the service of the nation to compel obedience to its laws" regardless of state compliance.[13] This decision reconfirmed the President's authority to utilize the military forces of the United States to execute the laws of the nation even under the restrictions set forth by the Posse Comitatus Act.

The use of military forces in civil affairs to restore peace and maintain state authority in accordance with the Constitution would continue with the onset of the 20th century. During the initial sixteen years of the 20th century, the executive branch employed military forces in what were mostly labor disputes. During this period, federal military forces emphasized their neutrality, practicing self-restraint and conformity to the letter of the Posse Comitatus Act and other applicable federal statutes. Administrations set out to demonstrate that the law could be applied impartially and that military intervention could be nonpartisan, well-coordinated, and smoothly executed.[14]

---

[13] Clayton D. Laurie and Ronald H. Cole, The Role of Federal Military Forces in Domestic Disorder 1877-1945, 150-151.

[14] Ibid., 221.

By 1917, in the dawn of a world war, the United States extended its power and authority to intervene in civil affairs in its effort to protect the nation from enemies both foreign and domestic. In May of 1917, Secretary of War Newton D. Baker unilaterally suspended the restraints placed upon the use of the military in civil affairs to include those within the Posse Comitatus Act. The Army was instructed to "respond to any call for military assistance ... for maintaining the domestic peace."[15] Over the next several years, local and state officials were able to directly request military support circumventing statutory procedures. Neither Congress nor the general public raised significant concerns and appeared to accept this policy as a necessary national security measure during a period of national emergency. Though hostilities had ended in Europe in November of 1918, Baker's policies continued to govern the use of the military in domestic affairs until Warren G. Harding took office as the 29th President of the United States in 1921 announcing a "return to normalcy."

The use of federal military forces to quell disorders and maintain the peace would dramatically decline in future years with the emergence of strengthened local and state police forces and capable National Guard units. It would not be until 1932, when rioting broke out in Washington, D.C. during the Bonus March, that the military would once again engage in another major domestic intervention.

In the midst of a worsening economic depression, the American public increasingly looked to the federal government for assistance. Much of the public did not believe that the economy would turn around without federal stimulation and increasingly

---

[15] Clayton D. Laurie and Ronald H. Cole, The Role of Federal Military Forces in Domestic Disorder 1877-1945, 230.

held President Hoover personally responsible for the depression.[16] The election of Franklin D. Roosevelt in November of 1932 was to bring about the social, political, and economic change to the United States the American public desired. Roosevelt's New Deal created the modern welfare state necessitating heavy government involvement for continued successful operation.[17] The intervention by the federal government in domestic affairs transitioned from the use of military force to diplomatic mediation and arbitration and left matters of quelling violence to local and state governments who in turn, relied primarily upon local and state law enforcement bodies.

As the United States entered into World War II, the civil-military policies governing the use of military forces in civil affairs remained intact and federal government intervention continued primarily through diplomatic means. In 1945, U.S. Army regulations would reflect the evolution and maturation of the government's application of military forces in civil affairs advising commanders that they should employ only such force as is necessary to accomplish their mission of restoring order and maintaining lawful authority.[18] The further development of doctrine and contingency plans, dealing with the employment of military forces in aiding civil authorities during domestic disturbances, greatly diminished concerns of both civil and military leaders regarding the legality of such interventions following the passage of the Posse Comitatus Act.[19]

---

[16] Kennesaw State University, "1932: Roosevelt Defeats Hoover," KSU, http://www.kennesaw.edu/pols/3380/pres/1932.html (accessed 25 February 2012).

[17] Clayton D. Laurie and Ronald H. Cole, The Role of Federal Military Forces in Domestic Disorder 1877-1945, 389.

[18] Ibid., 420-421.

[19] Ibid., 424.

In the wake of WWII and during the reorganization of the military services under the National Security Act of 1949, the Department of the Army was designated in 1953 as having "primary responsibility among the military services for rendering assistance to civil authorities in domestic disturbances" while the remaining services assumed a "collateral function for providing such assistance."[20]

In May of 1954, the Supreme Court in a landmark decision ruled in Brown v. Board of Education of Topeka that race segregation of public schools was unconstitutional. Opposition was swift to the decision with many states, predominantly in the South, denouncing the court's ruling. President Eisenhower, though supportive of the court's ruling for integration, declined to take federal action in its enforcement stating "I can't imagine any set of circumstances that would ever induce me to send Federal troops into ... any area to enforce the orders of a Federal court, because I believe that [the] common sense of America will never require it."[21] Progress in school desegregation languished due to the lack of both presidential and congressional support.

By 1957 though, Eisenhower's vision proved incorrect with developments unable to be contained by local and state intervention in Little Rock, Arkansas. To achieve integration of Little Rock's Central High School would take the combined efforts of both federalized National Guard and federal troops. Concerns over the President's authority to utilize federal troops during this crisis and violating the Posse Comitatus Act were addressed by Attorney General Herbert Brownell stating that "the President had acted

---

[20] Paul J. Scheips, *The Role of Federal Military Forces in Domestic Disorder 1945-1992* (Washington, DC: Center of Military History, 2005) 6.

[21] U.S. Government, *Public Papers of the Presidents of the United States: Dwight D. Eisenhower, 1957* (Washington, DC: U.S. Government Printing Office, 1958) 546.

with careful attention to the provisions of the law, which had never been intended by Congress to impair powers the chief executive possessed under existing statutes."[22]

Civil Rights and antiwar movements would sweep through the nation over the next two decades necessitating the need for federal government intervention by military force to maintain law and order and civil authority. In 1967, during the planning for the federal government's response to an antiwar protest on the grounds of the Pentagon, questions arose over the applicability of the Posse Comitatus Act in using National Guard forces in its various federal and state statuses. It was determined that National Guard forces within their state status could be appointed as special law enforcement bodies to assist local police forces in enforcing federal, state, and local laws citing Attorney General Caleb Cushing's 1854 opinion. In the Guard's federalized status however, the Posse Comitatus Act was believed to prohibit such action.[23] This interpretation of the act is yet another example of an attempt to further clarify the law and apply it within an environment transformed by ninety years of significant change.

In the years that followed, military forces continued to be used to quell riots across the nation. In the District of Columbia, Detroit, Chicago, and Baltimore riots, federal forces augmented local authorities, providing both personnel and logistical support. The intervention by the federal government followed a disciplined process in accordance with the laws governing such actions.

In 1968, following the assassination of Robert F. Kennedy, the Johnson administration became increasingly concerned with the internal security of the United

---

[22] Paul J. Scheips, The Role of Federal Military Forces in Domestic Disorder 1945-1992, 55.

[23] Ibid., 241.

States. In June of that year, Public Law 90-331 was ratified which required, upon the request of the Director of the United States Secret Service, all Federal Departments and agencies to "assist the Secret Service in the performance of its protective duties."[24] Assistant Attorney General William H. Rehnquist, speaking on behalf of the Department of Justice, declared that Public Law 90-331 was exempt from the restrictions established by the Posse Comitatus Act.

In 1971, the Department of Defense Directive 3025.12, *Employment of Military Resources in the Event of Civil Disturbances*, was revised and provided a number of exceptions to the Posse Comitatus Act "based upon the inherent legal right of the United States Government ... to insure the preservation of public order and the carrying out of governmental operations ... by force if necessary."[25] The first provided emergency authority to protect life or property while the second provided the authority to secure federal property and functions when there was a "need" for such protection and local authorities were incapable or unwilling to act.[26]

In 1973, events at Wounded Knee, South Dakota would once again bring about concerns surrounding the legalities of using military forces in domestic affairs under the provisions of the Posse Comitatus Act. Though military assistance was limited to the supply of equipment and advice to law enforcement authorities, the ensuing court opinions on whether military involvement in the matter violated the act varied widely and

---

[24] U.S. Congress, Senate, *Congressional Record 114*, 6 June 1968 (Washington, DC: Government Printing Office, 1968)16169-70.

[25] DOD Directive 3025.12, *Employment of Military Resources in the Event of Civil Disturbances*, 19 Aug 71(Washington, DC: Dept. of Defense, 1971).

[26] Paul J. Scheips, The Role of Federal Military Forces in Domestic Disorder 1945-1992, 418.

was often contradictory. In 1975, the South Dakota federal district court ruled in *U.S. vs. Red Feather* that the military role in the Wounded Knee event was not in violation to the Posse Comitatus Act. In making this ruling though, the court was required to further interpret the language of the Posse Comitatus Act and infer as to the intent of the law's drafters.

> The senators who drafted and debated the bill and President Hayes who signed the bill into law, were of the belief that 18 U.S.C. Sec. 1385 made unlawful the use of federal military troops in the active role of direct law enforcement or execution of process. Based upon the clear intent of Congress, this Court holds that the clause 'to execute the laws,' contained in 18 U.S.C. Sec. 1385, makes unlawful the use of federal military troops in an active role of direct law enforcement by civil law enforcement officers.
>
> Activities which constitute an active role in direct law enforcement are: arrest; seizure of evidence; search of a person; search of a building; investigation of crime; interviewing witnesses; pursuit of an escaped civilian prisoner; search of an area for a suspect or other like activities. Such use of federal military troops to 'execute the laws,' or as the Court has defined the clause, in 'an active role of direct law enforcement,' is unlawful under 18 U.S.C. Sec.1385...
>
> Activities which constitute a passive role . . . military personnel under orders to report on the necessity for military intervention; preparation of contingency plans to be used if military intervention is ordered; advice or recommendations given to civilian law enforcement officers by military personnel on tactics or logistics; presence of military personnel to deliver military material, equipment or supplies, to train local law enforcement officials on the proper use and care of such material or equipment, and to maintain such material or equipment; aerial photographic reconnaissance flights and other like activities. Such passive involvement of federal military troops which might indirectly aid civilian law enforcement is not made unlawful under 18 U.S.C. Sec 1385 ...[27]

The court opinioned that the Posse Comitatus Act was drafted "to eliminate the direct *active* use of federal troops by civil law enforcement officers," but that it was not intended "to prevent the use of ... materiel or equipment in aid of execution of the laws."[28] Though the Posse Comitatus Act does not contain this distinction, the court

---

[27] *U. S. v. Red Feather*, 392 F.Supp. 916 (1975)
http://www.icdc.com/~paulwolf/cointelpro/law/USvRedFeather392FSupp916.htm (accessed 26 November 2011).

[28] Ibid.

interpreted that the role of military forces in domestic affairs could be classified as either active or passive participation, the latter being permissible by the Posse Comitatus Act.

Two other cases arose from the Wounded Knee event that further clarified whether the use of military forces in domestic affairs would be considered a violation of the Posse Comitatus Act. In *United States vs. Jaramillo*, the court opinioned that it could be concluded that a violation of the Posse Comitatus Act may have taken place if the "use of any part of the Army or Air Force pervaded the activities of the [civilian law enforcement authorities]."[29] Though the court did not rule that any violation of the act took place, they believed that any use of military personnel (excluding equipment) that influenced civilian law enforcement activities, could be construed as a violation of the act. In *United States vs. McArthur*, the court opinioned that the analysis in Red Feather, as to whether or not a violation of the Posse Comitatus Act took place, was "too mechanical" and that in Jaramillo, the analysis required a judgment to be made from "too vague a standard." The court in McArthur focused on the Posse Comitatus Act's restriction against the use of a part of the Army or Air Force to "execute" the law. In response, it concluded that the use of military forces by civilian law enforcement officers would be a violation of the Posse Comitatus Act if their use subjected citizens to the "exercise of military power which was regulatory, proscriptive, or compulsory in nature, either presently or prospectively."[30] The court stated that, though the opinion in McArthur "was ultimately a factual determination, it was guided by legal assumptions

---

[29] *U.S. v. Jaramillo*, 380 F.Supp. 1375 (1974) http://174.123.24.242/leagle/xmlResult.aspx?xmldoc=19741755380FSupp1375_11575.xml&docbase=CSLWAR1-1950-1985 (accessed 30 November 2011).

[30] *U.S. v. McArthur*, 419 F.Supp. 186 (1976) http://174.123.24.242/leagle/xmlResult.aspx?xmldoc=1976605419FSupp186_1562.xml&docbase=CSLWAR1-1950-1985 (accessed 30 November 2011).

about the meaning of the posse comitatus statute."[31] The opinions of these three court cases would provide the federal government, which had long sought legal guidance in its application of military forces in civil affairs, a legal basis for such operations which would be used to govern the future employment of such forces.

By 1981, in an effort to increase Department of Defense and civilian law enforcement cooperation in combating the growing problems associated with illicit drugs, Congress approved specific language within the Department of Defense Authorization Act of 1982 to further clarify the Department's engagement with its civilian counterparts. The new law largely provided additional exemptions to the Posse Comitatus Act by authorizing the Defense Department to engage in information sharing, allow for the use, operation, and maintenance of Defense Department facilities and equipment, and provide for the training and advising of civilian officials.

Additionally the new law, in accordance with the court's opinion established in *United States v. Red Feather*, directed the Secretary of Defense to issue regulations restricting military personnel from actively participating in law enforcement activities. In April of 1982, the Department of Defense issued regulations to limit direct military involvement in specified law enforcement activities to include participation in an interdiction of a vehicle, vessel, or aircraft, a search and seizure, arrest, or other similar activity unless otherwise authorized by law.[32] Further regulations imposed an extension of the Posse Comitatus Act to cover military operations outside of the United States as

---

[31] Ibid.

[32] Gary Felicetti and John Luce, "The Posse Comitatus Act: Setting the Record Straight on 124 Years of Mischief and Misunderstanding Before Any More Damage is Done,", 152.

well as making the act applicable to the remaining services (Navy and Marine Corps) which had originally been precluded from the Posse Comitatus Act.

These Defense regulations were perceived by many to be based upon an overly restrictive interpretation of the Posse Comitatus Act, further adding to the confusion over its modern understanding. The Department, having significantly expanded the scope of the original Posse Comitatus Act, ultimately instituted a version of the Act explicitly rejected by the Senate in 1878. [33] The Defense regulations became an extension of the Posse Comitatus Act providing additional layers to the ambiguous law making it more difficult to distinguish between the original Act and subsequent interpretations by the Department's regulations.

In 1988, concerns over border enforcement and a perception of America losing its war on drugs prompted Congress to enact specific language within the Defense Authorization Act of 1989 which significantly increased the armed forces role in drug interdiction. The Defense Act required the Department of Defense "to plan and budget for the effective detection and monitoring of all potential aerial and maritime threats to the national security."[34] The act also designated the Department as the lead federal agency for the detection and monitoring of aerial and maritime transit of illegal drugs into the country.[35]

---

[33] Gary Felicetti and John Luce, "The Posse Comitatus Act: Setting the Record Straight on 124 Years of Mischief and Misunderstanding Before Any More Damage is Done,", 154.

[34] U.S. Congress, *H.R. CONF. REP. NO. 100-989*, U.S.C.C.A.N. 2575 (Washington, D.C.: U.S. G.P.O, 1988) 447.

[35] Ibid.

The 1989 Defense Authorization Act provided for the use of Department personnel and equipment in intercepting vessels and aircraft outside of the United States and allowed for the greater delegation of authorities in providing military assistance in cases of emergencies. In addition, Congress identified any civilian agency enforcing customs, drugs, immigration, and terrorism laws could receive enhanced military assistance. With the Iraqi invasion of Kuwait in 1990, the Department became increasingly disinterested in expanding its current responsibilities and its role in counter drug enforcement under the 1989 Defense Authorization Act was predominantly rejected.[36] Though the act was clearly intended to increase the Department's passive participation in law enforcement, Defense regulations restricting its assistance remained unchanged.

The confusion over the Posse Comitatus Act and Department regulations had come to a point in April of 1992 when mass rioting, resulting in 54 deaths, over 2000 injured, $900 million in lost property, and over 8,600 arrests fell upon the city of Los Angeles.[37] Initial National Guard response under the governor's authority significantly bolstered civilian law enforcement efforts to quell the disorder. Guard personnel assisted in patrolling public areas, managing traffic check points, and protecting emergency workers and sensitive areas.[38] Although rioting had begun to subside, political leadership remained skeptical that current efforts were capable of completely squelching the

---

[36] Stephen M. Duncan, Citizen Warriors: America's National Guard and Reserve Forces & Politics of National Security (Novato, CA: Presidio Press, 1997) 176-180.

[37] Paul J. Scheips, The Role of Federal Military Forces in Domestic Disorder 1945-1992, 448.

[38] Susan Rosegrant, *The Flawed Emergency Response to the 1992 Los Angeles Riots* (Cambridge: Kennedy School of Government, 2000) 16.

disorder. At the request of the California governor, President Bush ordered 4,000 active-duty Army and Marines into Los Angeles and federalized the California National Guard. Though the Posse Comitatus Act did not apply to the use of military forces under executive order, military personnel were instructed that they were no longer authorized to perform such civil law enforcement duties such as those that the National Guard forces were currently engaged in to bolster civilian law enforcement efforts. This had a significant impact on the mission types that military personnel could engage in and resulted in the plummeting of support request approvals by 80 percent.[39] There continues to be some debate as to the true reasons for the military's disengagement from law enforcement missions within the Los Angeles Riots, but it is evident that the applicability of the Posse Comitatus Act remains at its center.

---

[39] Christopher M. Schnaubelt, "Lessons in Command and Control from the Los Angeles Riots," *Parameters*, US Army War College Quarterly (Summer 1997): 88-109, http://www.carlisle.army.mil/USAWC/Parameters/Articles/97summer/schnau.htm (accessed 18 December 2011).

CHAPTER 4:

THE PCA POST-9/11

Over the next several years, the use of military forces in domestic affairs was predominantly employed without much incident, abiding by the Posse Comitatus Act and supporting Defense regulations. It would not be until the 2001 terror attacks that the Posse Comitatus Act and the use of the armed forces in civil affairs would once again become a predominate topic of discussion. In the wake of the attacks, in an environment fueled by raw emotion, many voiced their concerns that the federal government was not doing enough to protect its citizens. Many believed that the attacks had forever changed the American way of life and therefore sought bold changes to the restrictions placed on civilian-military cooperation.

> Since the tragic, unforeseen terrorist attacks on September 11, our nation must reexamine our military doctrine . . . The world has dramatically changed; our way of life has forever changed. Should [the Posse Comitatus Act] now be changed to enable our military to more fully join other domestic assets in this war against terrorism? . . . In view of recent events and the unique capabilities which the armed forces can bring to emergency situations, I request the Department review this issue and make any recommendations for changes.[1]
>
> Former Senator and Chairman of the Senate Armed Services Committee John Warner
> October 2001

The September 2001 Quadrennial Defense Review Report affirmed the strategic role the military serves in the internal defense of the United States. The report identified that the purpose of the U.S. Armed Forces is to protect and advance U.S. national

---

[1] Gerald J. Manley, "The Posse Comitatus Act Post-9/11: Time for a Change?" National War College, Ft. Belvoir Defense Technical Information Center (January 2003) 16. http://www.dtic.mil/cgi-bin/GetTRDoc?AD=ADA441745 (accessed: 29 February 2012) Citing "John Warner, Letter to Secretary of Defense Donald Rumsfeld, 11 October 2001".

interests. The first of these national interests is to ensure U.S. security and freedom of action to include the safety of U.S. citizens at home and abroad.[2]

Prior to the establishment of the Department of Homeland Security in November of 2002, the Bush Administration completed its comprehensive national strategy for the new department. The National Strategy for Homeland Security identified the need in protecting civil liberties and individual freedoms, but recognized that liberty cannot exist in the absence of governmental restraint.[3] The document further identified that existing laws in protecting the homeland may be inadequate in light of the 2001 terrorist attacks and that revisions to existing laws or the creation of new laws may be required to better ensure the protection of the country.

> Federal law prohibits military personnel from enforcing the law within the United States except as expressly authorized by the Constitution or an Act of Congress. The threat of catastrophic terrorism requires a thorough review of the laws permitting the military to act within the United States in order to determine whether domestic preparedness and response efforts would benefit from greater involvement of military personnel and, if so, how.[4]
>
> President George W. Bush, 2002

Within the 2002 National Security Strategy, President Bush identified that "defending our Nation against its enemies is the first and fundamental commitment of the Federal Government... To defeat this threat, we must make use of every tool in our arsenal – military power, better homeland defenses, law enforcement, intelligence, and vigorous efforts to cut off terrorist financing."[5]

---

[2] U.S. Government. *Quadrennial Defense Review Report*, 2001 (Washington, D.C.: Government Printing Office, September 2001) 2.

[3] U.S. President. *The National Strategy for Homeland Security*, 2002 (Washington, D.C.: Government Printing Office, July 2002) 48.

[4] Ibid.

[5] U.S. President. *The National Security Strategy of the United States of America*, 2002 (Washington, D.C.: Government Printing Office, September 2002) 3.

To properly assume these responsibilities of defending the homeland, the Department of Defense established the United States Northern Command (NORTHCOM) on 1 Oct 2002. NORTHCOM's initial mission was stated as "homeland defense and civil support, specifically: conduct operations to deter, prevent, and defeat threats and aggression aimed at the United States, its territories, and interests within the assigned area of responsibilities; as directed by the President or Secretary of Defense, provide military assistance to civil authorities including consequence management operations."[6] The establishment of NORTHCOM and NORTHCOM's subsequent mission statement signified a major change in the Department's perceived role in the domestic defense mission.

Aware that NORTHCOM's mission would envelope new responsibilities subject to the restrictions of the Posse Comitatus Act and other such laws, the unified command set out to clarify its mission sets by differentiating between those of homeland security and homeland defense. Determining when the Posse Comitatus Act would apply would fundamentally rest on if the mission was one of homeland security or of homeland defense.

---

[6] James R. Weber, "The Posse Comitatus Act of 1878: An Historical Perspective and Implications for Homeland Defense," Strategic Studies Institute, U.S. Army War College (April 2003): 14, http://www.dtic.mil/dtic/tr/fulltext/u2/a420136.pdf (accessed 12 February 2012) citing United States Northern Command, 3 October 2002.

Homeland Security:

Homeland Security is the prevention, preemption, and deterrence of, and defense against, aggression targeted at U.S. territory, sovereignty, domestic population, and infrastructure as well as the management of the consequences of such aggression and other domestic emergencies.[7]

Homeland Defense:

Homeland Defense is the protection of U.S. territory, domestic population and critical infrastructure against military attacks emanating from outside the United States.[8]

NORTHCOM continued to divorce itself from those missions within the scope of homeland security and assume less substantial domestic support roles. The command further stated that "in understanding the difference between HLS [Homeland Security] and HLD [Homeland Defense], it is important to understand that NORTHCOM is a military organization whose operations within the United States are governed by law, including the Posse Comitatus Act that prohibits direct military involvement in law enforcement activities. Thus, NORTHCOM's missions are limited to military homeland defense and civil support to lead federal agencies."[9] Since a significant portion of the homeland security mission is contained within the "law enforcement" purview and no additional exclusions to the Posse Comitatus Act were granted with the establishment of NORTHCOM, the role of military forces in domestic affairs has remained unchanged. Though the establishment of NORTHCOM has not furthered military interaction in domestic affairs, it has provided a single entity by which support efforts are now

---

[7] Geoffrey Crawford, "Posse Comitatus Act: Clarification is Necessary to Support Homeland Defense," US Army Command and General Staff College (June 2004): 37, http://www.dtic.mil/cgi-bin/GetTRDoc?AD=ADA428698 (accessed 12 February 2012) citing United States Northern Command, 11 September 2003.

[8] Ibid.

[9] Ibid.

coordinated between the Department of Defense and domestic agencies requiring military assistance.

Today's NORTHCOM mission statement significantly differs from its original by excluding its direct role in the defense of the homeland and subjecting itself to one of providing limited support to other federal agencies.

USNORTHCOM mission statement October 2002:

The Command's mission is homeland defense and civil support, specifically: conduct operations to deter, prevent, and defeat threats and aggression aimed at the United States, its territories, and interests within the assigned area of responsibilities; as directed by the President or Secretary of Defense, provide military assistance to civil authorities including consequence management operations.[10]

USNORTHCOM mission statement January 2012:

USNORTHCOM partners to conduct homeland defense, civil support and security cooperation to defend and secure the United States and its interests.[11]

---

[10] James R. Weber, "The Posse Comitatus Act of 1878: An Historical Perspective and Implications for Homeland Defense,", 14.

[11] U.S. Government, "United States Northern Command: Defending our Homeland," USNORTHCOM, http://www.northcom.mil/About/index.html (accessed 16 January 2012).

CHAPTER 5:

THE PATH FORWARD

> Unless we act to prevent it, a new wave of terrorism, potentially involving the world's most destructive weapons, looms in America's future. It is a challenge as formidable as any ever faced by our Nation. Today's terrorists can strike at any place, at any time, and with virtually any weapon. Securing the American homeland is a challenge of monumental scale and complexity. But the U.S. government has no more important mission.[12]

The National Strategy for Homeland Security, 2002

The United States will likely experience further attacks in its future. It is not a question of *if*, but more of *when*. A decade has passed since the attacks of September 11th and the United States continues to remain unprepared to prevent or respond to such attacks to its homeland. Is it appropriate to erode the authority of America's largest and most capable element of national power in protecting the homeland as threats get closer to our nation's shores? What is the role of our military forces? Is it first and foremost to fight our battles and win our wars abroad or that of defending the homeland? Many would argue that the battles and the war have come home and that a shift in strategy is required.

Though we are a nation of laws, we cannot allow ourselves to become paralyzed by these laws and allow them to restrict our ability to act both in times of crisis as well as in times of peace. Our enemies will continue to adapt to our legal formalities and exploit those areas that are neither black nor white. The Posse Comitatus Act has proven to be such a law that provides much confusion and ultimately impedes our nation's ability to

---

[12] U.S. President. The National Strategy for Homeland Security, 2002, 1.

respond to threats. It is safe to say that our enemies do not recognize the artificial construct between homeland security and that of defense. Threats will continue to transcend geographic borders and organizational domains. In a hearing before the Committee of Governmental Affairs on the development of the Department of Homeland Security, former Senator Gary Hart stated that "in the event of a catastrophic attack of some kind, obviously, every asset of this country is going to come into play. Nobody's going to be worried about the niceties of the Posse Comitatus Act."[13] History has shown us that the Posse Comitatus Act has always been a law in which political and military leaders have disregarded its restrictive language in times of necessity.

The current Department of Defense strategy for securing the homeland is to deter, counter, and defeat threats abroad before they reach our shores. As noted in the National Strategy for Homeland Security, the enemies we face are versatile, shrewd, and capable. We may not always be able to address each of these threats before they find their way to our shores. It is imperative that our nation's many departments whose responsibilities lie with the preservation and security of the nation be fully integrated and any laws or policies restricting this endeavor be reviewed and potentially changed or even repealed.

As this paper illustrates, the military element of national power has had a long and decisive role in the domestic affairs of this nation. Prior to and since the borders of this great nation reaching from the Atlantic to the Pacific Oceans, U.S. military forces have been at the forefront to protect the country from both internal and external threats. The oath of enlistment states that service members "will support and defend the Constitution

---

[13] Congress, Senate, Committee on Governmental Affairs, *The Homeland Security Department: Hearing before the Committee on Governmental Affairs,* 107th Congress, 2nd Session, 20 June 2002 (Washington, D.C.: Government Printing Office, June 2002) 63.

of the United States against all enemies, foreign and domestic." So the question is what has changed?

Until our nation's borders can be secured and the flow of information, goods, and people properly controlled, the United States homeland will continue to remain susceptible to those wishing us harm. Despite the many steps taken to secure our nation since the attacks of September 11th, America's borders remain porous and its homeland ominously exposed. The security of the borders of the United States must be of the highest priority. If the United States is unable to secure its borders, it will remain incapable of providing a secure homeland to its citizens. The numerous threats which are exposed and countered each day in this country will not further our nation's security unless we are able to deny access by new and emerging threats into this country.

Not only are the physical borders of the United States of great concern, the almost borderless cyber environment adds a whole other dimension which provides enormous opportunities for exploitation. Over the last several decades, the United States' dependency on sophisticated networks to move people, food, cargo, energy, money, and information has grown significantly with little attention paid to its security.[14] Today, the most capable agency in dealing with this problem is the National Security Agency. The National Security Agency though is an agency under the Department of Defense and therefore is subject to those restrictions placed upon it by the Posse Comitatus Act. Cyber programs are fairly new and many issues are still being resolved by the various departments that have responsibilities within its environment. In September of 2010, the Department of Defense and the Department of Homeland Security entered into a

---

[14] Stephen E. Flynn, America the Vulnerable, How Our Government Is Failing to Protect Us from Terrorism (New York: Harper Collins, 2004) 5.

Memorandum of Agreement allowing for the increase in interdepartmental collaboration in strategic planning for the nation's cyber security, mutual support for cyber security capabilities development, and synchronization of current operational cyber security mission activities.[15] Though the agreement is clear about the chain of command of the employees from the two departments, it poses many questions regarding the separation of military and civilian domains required by the Posse Comitatus Act.

The Goldwater-Nichols Department of Defense Reorganization Act of 1986 was brought about as the nation could no longer afford individual service capabilities. The Goldwater-Nichols Act in turn, forced the services to operate jointly. It is impractical to believe that the nation can further afford to separate the capabilities of the Department of Defense from those of its civilian counterparts in defending this country. In order to move forward in our nation's security, especially within the current constrained financial environment, the United States will be required to find efficiencies within its institutions and dissolve the barriers that bar integration and interoperability. The United States can ill afford to accept a quasi-solution to the protection of its people.

Out of the $612.3 billion spent in Fiscal Year 2011 under the continuing resolution between the Department of Defense, the Department of Homeland Security, and the Department of Justice, 86% of the funding was provided to the Department of Defense. The remaining 14% was provided to the remaining two departments predominantly responsible for the security of the homeland. In regards to personnel, the Department of Defense is over fifteen times larger than the Department of Homeland

---

[15] U.S. Government, "Memorandum of Agreement Between the Department of Homeland Security and the Department of Defense Regarding Cybersecurity," http://www.defense.gov/news/d20101013moa.pdf (accessed 22 January 2012).

Security and the Department of Justice combined. Given the stated priorities of our nation as identified within the National Security Strategy, there seems to be a disparity between national resource allocations and national interests. One would assume that the majority of a nation's resources would be focused on its highest priority and since the Department of Defense's role in Homeland Defense is limited to the protection of U.S. territory, domestic population and critical infrastructure *against military attacks* emanating from outside the United States, this disparity should be significantly less.[16]

Budget (Billions)

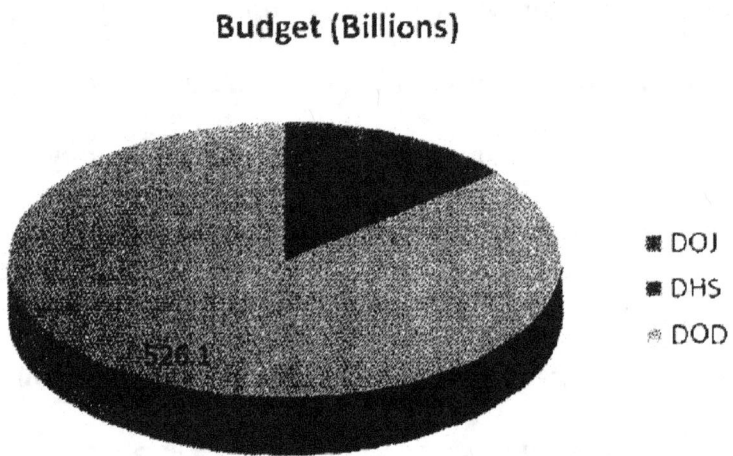

Figure 1. Fiscal Year 2011 Budget. Source: Department of Defense Fiscal Year 2012 Budget Request, http://comptroller.defense.gov/defbudget/fy2012/FY2012_Budget_Request_Overview_Book.pdf (accessed 25 February 2012) 1-1; Homeland Security FY 2012 Budget in Brief http://www.dhs.gov/xlibrary/assets/budget-bib-fy2012.pdf (accessed 25 February 2012) 3; Department of Justice FY 2012 Budget and Performance Summary http://www.justice.gov/jmd/2012summary/pdf/fy12-bud-summary-request-performance.pdf (accessed 25 February 2012) 3.

---

[16] Geoffrey Crawford, "Posse Comitatus Act: Clarification is Necessary to Support Homeland Defense,". 37.

Personnel (Thousands)

- DOJ
- DHS
- DOD

Figure 2. Fiscal Year 2011 Departmental Personnel Statistics. Source: Statistical Information Analysis Division (SIAD) Civilian Employment and Military Personnel Statistics, http://siadapp.dmdc.osd.mil/personnel/CIVILIAN/fy2011/december2010/december2010.pdf http://siadapp.dmdc.osd.mil/personnel/MILITARY/history/hst1109.pdf (accessed 16 February 2012); Homeland Security FY 2012 Budget in Brief http://www.dhs.gov/xlibrary/assets/budget-bib-fy2012.pdf (accessed 25 February 2012) 171; Department of Justice FY 2012 Budget and Performance Summary http://www.justice.gov/jmd/2012summary/pdf/fy12-bud-summary-request-performance.pdf (accessed 25 February 2012) 3.

It is understandable that as civilian agencies have matured and have become more capable in effectively executing the enforcement of law, the need for military forces in domestic affairs diminishes. Many would argue though that the complete divorcement of military forces from a direct role in domestic affairs is premature. Federal, state and local agencies responsible for the daily welfare of citizens within the United States have been capable in providing for their protection by their ability to enforce the laws of the nation, but not without substantial risk.

Domestic law enforcement agencies remain incapable of managing the various threats posed by significant events. The 1992 mass rioting in Los Angles, the terror attacks on September 11th, 2001 and Hurricane Katrina in 2005 quickly overwhelmed

53

domestic law enforcement capacity. The ability of domestic law enforcement agencies to successfully operate outside of what one might consider "normal operations" is simply inadequate. Domestic law enforcement agencies remain incapable of effectively responding to the consequences of such events.

Most would agree that the inclusion of Department of Defense assets into the "normal operations" of domestic law enforcement agencies would not guarantee the complete denial of significant threats to our homeland or the adequate response to the consequences of those threats, but the additional capabilities and the capacity to manage such threats would significantly decrease the current risks being assumed. Water and food supplies, chemical plants, energy grids and pipelines, bridges, tunnels, ports, and the millions of cargo containers that carry most of the goods U.S. consumers depend on remain areas of high risk in which our enemies will continue to exploit.[17] The United States will remain incapable in securing such areas unless it employs a whole of government approach. This approach will necessitate the integration of all areas of the Department of Defense with those civilian departments responsible for the security of the Homeland.

---

[17] Stephen E. Flynn, America the Vulnerable, How Our Government Is Failing to Protect Us from Terrorism, 2.

CONCLUSION

It was this author's intention to provide the reader with an analysis of the historical context of the Posse Comitatus Act and dispel many of the false beliefs surrounding the original intent of the 45th Congress. The Posse Comitatus Act was initially created to assist Southern states in denying black freedoms. Today, the act is viewed by many as a guardian of American freedoms against undue oppression by the federal government's military arm. Many authorities have attributed the provisions of the Posse Comitatus Act as being based upon Constitutional foundations. Though the Constitution prohibits the quartering of soldiers in private homes without consent and places the control of the military squarely in the hands of its civilian authorities, the Constitution makes no assertion restricting the use of military forces in the enforcement of civilian law. Many argue that policymakers must understand the Posse Comitatus Act before they are able to *fix* it, but after 133 years, we are no further along in this endeavor. In fact, many would argue that the current interpretation of the Posse Comitatus Act is almost the exact opposite from what its authors intended.

Military forces in domestic affairs have traditionally been seen by many Americans as intrusive and dangerous to individual freedoms. "When the government wishes to deprive its citizens of freedom, and reduce them to slavery, it generally makes use of a standing army."[1] Many have struggled with the question of how to maintain a capable military while at the same time not losing civilian control over such a powerful

---

[1] Max Farrand and David Maydole Matteson, *The Records of the Federal Convention of 1787*, Vol. 3 (New Haven, CT: Yale University Press, 1937) 209.

body. The limitation of the federal government's power to regulate and enforce its will

upon the people has always had popular support within the United States. The

Constitution provides provisions to limit the authority of the control of the military body

by any one office, but does not impose restrictions toward using the military to enforce

civil laws. As such, the Posse Comitatus Act is seen as the guiding principle governing

military preservation and enforcement of civilian law. The Posse Comitatus Act has

become a symbolic instrument of civilian supremacy over its military forces. A repeal of

the act would be formidable as it would invoke many emotions, however leaving the act

in place will only continue to impede our country's ability to provide for the security of

its citizens and hamper a holistic response to the consequences of future significant

events.

Though the intentions behind the act are sound, one must reexamine our nation's

priorities within the context of our current national security environment. This paper may

have become more about resources than it has about responsibilities and the laws that

govern them. It is imperative that we make every effort to ensure that our nation's

limited resources are in the right place based upon our priorities. The President's

National Security Strategy identifies the security of the United States, its citizens, and

U.S. allies and partners as its primary national security interest.[2] In light of this, the

majority of U.S. resources should be focused in advancing this national interest. Until we

change our National Security Strategy and balance the capacities and capabilities of each

of the departments so they may be able to properly assume their responsibilities and

---

[2] U.S. President. *The National Strategy for Homeland Security*, 2010
(Washington, D.C.: Government Printing Office, May 2010) 17.

effectively and efficiently carry them out, the Department of Defense will continue to be the instrument of choice to execute traditionally non-DOD responsibilities.

The Posse Comitatus Act though has created an environment in which political and military leaders are reluctant to engage due to their uncertainty of the act's provisions. Little formal education of the requirements set forth by the Posse Comitatus Act is given to our leaders; most of which will need to have a have a basic understanding of the act at some point in their career. This is a shortcoming which must be addressed. It is vital that those who the American people have entrusted with their welfare understand the authorities and restrictions placed upon them so they may act accordingly and decisively in the performance of their duties.

Exacerbating this problem, court opinions and departmental directives further add to the current quagmire behind the confusion surrounding the Posse Comitatus Act. Since the act's inception in 1878, Congress has steadily increased the military's role in regulatory action and law enforcement. In doing so, the Posse Comitatus Act has become plagued with exceptions adding complexity to an already complex law.

Such cases as the 1975 Wounded Knee opinions have led to an artificial construct deeming what is appropriate and inappropriate military action in civil law enforcement. Though the court's opinions were said to have been based upon the language and intent of the Posse Comitatus Act, nowhere within the act or the congressional transcripts of the 45th Congress is there a distinction between active and passive military participation. As the act is inherently overly broad, much has been constructed to clarify its meaning, sometimes in detriment to what many scholars and historians believe to be the act's true intent.

Exceptions to the act such as the Department of Defense's role in counterdrug operations have led to various cases where the involvement of military forces would not be authorized under the restrictions of the Posse Comitatus Act without a nexus to illicit drugs. This has steered many agencies that have had a need for the capabilities and expertise of military forces to be somewhat "creative" in articulating that a drug connection exists within their operations. These types of exceptions will continue to undermine the foundation of the act and its legitimacy. Many contend that these exceptions exist in an effort to balance our military's role in domestic affairs, yet often they only further complicate matters and invite argument rather than resolution.[3]

Many proponents of the Posse Comitatus Act view the act as providing shelter against the misuse of our military forces and the protection of their core competencies. It will be imperative that our military forces retain their core competencies and be placed in such conditions that would best mimic their normal operating environment. Most soldiers are not trained in law enforcement and their use of force lies at the extreme end of the spectrum. "Soldiers are taught to violently and effectively destroy the enemy, and their training does not include sensitivity to constitutional limitations on search, seizure, and the use of reasonable force."[4] This viewpoint is somewhat parochial and dated in today's context of U.S. forces effectively engaged in peacekeeping and humanitarian

---

[3] Donald J. Currier, "The Posse Comitatus Act: A Harmless Relic from the Post-Reconstruction Era or a Legal Impediment to Transformation," Strategic Studies Institute, U.S. Army War College (September 2003): 15 http://www.strategicstudiesinstitute.army.mil/pdffiles/pub249.pdf (accessed 23 January 2012).

[4] John Flock, "The Legality of United States Military Operations Along the United States-Mexico Border," *Southwestern Journal of Law and Trade in the Americas* 5, no. 2 (1998): 454.

missions throughout the globe. Service members will be required to train for peacetime operations within the territorial boundaries of the United States while fully understanding the authorities and restrictions placed upon them.

Many would argue that the National Guard should be the instrument of choice when military forces are required in domestic affairs as they are not subject to the restrictions of the Posse Comitatus Act while in state status. Limited resources, cross-border jurisdictional issues, and unity of command problems make the National Guard incapable of executing the National Security Strategy within the territorial borders of the United States.[5] If the National Guard were to be federalized, these issues would be resolved, but would be restricted in engaging in law enforcement activities due to the misapplication of the Posse Comitatus Act when their state status changes.

As outlined throughout this paper, not only does the legal foundation exist to use our nation's military forces to enforce civilian law, but prior to and since the enactment of the Posse Comitatus Act, we have employed these forces throughout our nation's history within this capacity. For 133 years, the exceedingly ambiguous Posse Comitatus Act has been misinterpreted and twisted into almost the exact opposite of what its authors intended. It has denied, in contrast to its original intent, the citizens of the United States the utmost protection by their federal government by denying its largest and most capable element of national power from protecting the homeland. The Federal Government will need to effectively utilize the combined resources of its numerous departments in order to accomplish this endeavor.

---

[5] Donald J. Currier, "The Posse Comitatus Act: A Harmless Relic from the Post-Reconstruction Era or a Legal Impediment to Transformation,", 14.

Unless the Posse Comitatus Act and subsequent regulations are addressed, our nation's ability to fully utilize the whole of government to defeat the current threats to our national security cannot be facilitated. The United States can ill-afford to continue to rely upon geography as its largest security asset. The severity of another attack to our homeland like those of 9/11 would be catastrophic to our nation's welfare. The probability of such an attack is looming. America must be willing to mobilize at home in order to confront the threats placed before it. The logic of defeating our nation's threats abroad before they reach our shores is sound yet has proven to be impractical. The U.S. homeland remains vulnerable, its borders providing little protection against those wishing it harm. As worldwide networks that support international trade and travel become more open and the level of cross-border activities increase, the opportunities for exploitation grows exponentially.[6]

Understanding that the resources of the United States are limited, the nation must address where it will focus its wealth and where it will assume risk. It can be inferred that given our present budget environment, our nation's ability to grow its resources to address additional areas of interest is unrealistic. Therefore, given that the nation's priority being the security of the homeland and its citizens, the preponderance of its resources should be applied against achieving this interest. The nation must not assume risk in this area. This will require the United States to accept risk in other areas by adjusting the focus of its limited resources accordingly.

It is proposed that the United States fully integrate its defense forces with its civilian departments if it wishes to prevent and respond to the threats presently posed to

---

[6] Stephen E. Flynn, America the Vulnerable, How Our Government Is Failing to Protect Us from Terrorism, 5.

its homeland. The Posse Comitatus Act has become a direct impediment to achieving this integration. Our ability to maintain separate departments with individual missions is not only inefficient and ineffective, but financially unviable. Currently, the misinterpretation of the Posse Comitatus Act and the addition of subsequent restrictions and exceptions have created an artificial divide between our nation's departments and in turn, have degraded our ability to properly protect the homeland. It is not sufficient to simply annul these restrictions and exceptions, whose language has captured much of what has been misconstrued about the Posse Comitatus Act, as this would merely leave an ambiguous law in place clearing the way for future misinterpretation. The Posse Comitatus Act and those regulations that are perceived to be based upon it need to be rescinded and replaced with new language that clearly identifies the terms in which the use of our military forces enhances Homeland Security while protecting civil liberties.

BIBLIOGRAPHY

Baldwin, Leland D. *Whiskey Rebels: The Story of a Frontier Uprising.* Pittsburgh: The University of Piottsburgh Press, 1939.

Brewer, E. Cobham. *Dictionary of Phrase and Fable.* Philadelphia: Henry Altemus Co. , 1898.

Brinkerhoff, John R. "The Posse Comitatus Act and Homeland Security." *Journal of Homeland Security,* 2002: 1-8.

Coakley, Robert W. *The Role of Federal Military Forces in Domestic Disorder 1789-1878.* Washington: Center of Military History, U.S. Army, Washington, D.C, 1988.

Commager, Henry Steel. *Documents of American History.* New York: Appleton-Century-Crofts, 1963.

Congress, Senate, Committee on Governmental Affairs. *The Homeland Security Department: Hearing before the Committee on Governmental Affairs.* Washington, D.C.: Government Printing Office, 20 June 2002.

Constitution Society. *Militia Act of 1792.* May 2, 1792. http://www.constitution.org/mil/mil_act_1792.htm (accessed October 15, 2011).

—. *The Judiciary Act of 1789.* September 24, 1789. http://www.constitution.org/uslaw/judiciary_1789.htm (accessed October 15, 2011).

Cooper, Jerry M. *The Army and civil disorder: Federal military intervention in labor disputes, 1877-1900.* Westport, Conn: Greenwood Press, 1980.

Cornell University Law School. *Legal Information Institute.* June 18, 1878. http://www.law.cornell.edu/uscode/18/usc_sec_18_00001385----000-.html (accessed October 30, 2011).

Crawford, Geoffrey. "Posse Comitatus Act: Clarification is Necessary to Support Homeland Defense." June 17, 2004. http://www.dtic.mil/cgi-bin/GetTRDoc?AD=ADA428698 (accessed February 12, 2012).

Currier, Donald J. "The Posse Comitatus Act: A Harmless Relic from the Post-Reconstruction Era or a Legal Impediment to Transformation? ." September 2003. http://www.strategicstudiesinstitute.army.mil/pdffiles/pub249.pdf (accessed January 23, 2012).

Department of Defense, Office of the Executive Secretary. *Annual Report to the President and the Congress.* Informational, Washington: U.S. Government Printing Office, 1998.

DOD Directive 3025.12. *Employment of Military Resources in the Event of Civil Disturbances, 19 Aug 71.* National Government Publication, Washington, DC: Dept. of Defense, 1971.

Duncan, Stephen M. *Citizen Warriors: America's National Guard and Reserve Forces & Politics of National Security.* Navato, CA: Presidio Press, 1997.

Farrand, Max and David Maydole Matteson. *The Records of the Federal Convention of 1787, Vol 3.* New Haven, CT: Yale University Press, 1937.

Felicetti, Gary and John Luce. "The Posse Comitatus Act: Setting the Record Straight on 124 Years of Mischief and Misunderstaning Before Any More Damage is Done." *Military Law Review,* 2003: 86-183.

Flock, John. "Notes and Comments: The Legality of the United States Military Operations Along the United States-Mexico Border." *Southwestern Journal of Law and Trade in the Americas,* 1998: 453-476.

Flynn, Stephen E. *America the Vulnerable, How Our Government Is Failing to Protect Us from Terrorism.* New York: Harper Collins, 2004.

Foner, Eric. *Reconstruction: America's Unfinished Revolution, 1863-1877.* New York: Harper & Row, 1988.

Patton Jr, George S. "Federal Troops in Domestic Disturbances." *The Patton Society.* November 1932. http://www.pattonhq.com/textfiles/federal.html (accessed October 9, 2011).

Kennesaw State University. *1932: Roosevelt Defeats Hoover.* n.d. http://www.kennesaw.edu/pols/3380/pres/1932.html (accessed February 25, 2012).

Kohn, Richard H. *Eagle and Sword.* New York: The Free Press, 1975.

Laurie, Clayton D. and Ronald H. Cole, *The Role of Federal Military Forces in Domestic Disordsers, 1877-1945.* Washington: Center of Military History, U.S. Army, Washington, D.C., 1997.

Manley, Gerald J. "The Posse Comitatus Act Post-9/11: A Time for a Change." *National War College.* January 2003. http://www.dtic.mil/cgi-bin/GetTRDoc?AD=ADA441745 (accessed February 29, 2012).

Mount, Steve. *U.S. Constitution - Amendment 14.* July 9, 1868. http://www.usconstitution.net/xconst_Am14.html (accessed November 6, 2011).

National Center for Public Policy Research. *Fugitive Slave Act 1850.* September 18, 1850. http://www.nationalcenter.org/FugitiveSlaveAct.html (accessed October 16, 2011).

National Intelligence Council. *Report of the National Intelligence Council's 2020 Project.* Compulation, Washington: Government Printing Office, 2004.

PBS. *1866 Civil Rights Act.* April 9, 1866. http://www.pbs.org/wgbh/amex/reconstruction/activism/ps_1866.html (accessed October 30, 2011).

Rosegrant, Susan. *The Flawed Emergency Response to the 1992 Los Angeles Riots.* Cambridge: Kennedy School of Government, 2000.

San Diego State University. *Insurrection Act, 1807.* March 3, 1807. http://www-rohan.sdsu.edu/dept/polsciwb/brianl/docs/1807InsurrectionAct.pdf (accessed October 16, 2011).

Scheips, Paul J. *The Role of Federal Military Forces in Domestic Disorders, 1945-1992.* Washington, D.C.: Center of Military History, United States Army, 2005.

Schnaubelt, Christopher M. "Lessons in Command and Control from the Los Angeles Riots." *Parameters, US Army War College Quarterly*, Summer 1997: 88-109.

U.S. Congress, Senate. *Congressional Record 114.* Washington, D.C.: Government Printing Office, 1968.

—. *H.R. CONF. REP. NO. 100-989.* Congressional Report, Washington, D.C.: U.S. G.P.O, 1988.

U.S. Government. *Constitution of the United States.* June 21, 1788. www.archives.gov/exhibits/charters/constitution.htm (accessed October 9, 2011).

—. "The Charters of Freedom," Archives, www.archives.gov/exhibits/charters/constitution.html (accessed 9 October 2011).

—. "Memorandum of Agreement Between the Department of Homeland Security and the Department of Defense Regarding Cybersecurity." September 27, 2010. http://www.defense.gov/news/d20101013moa.pdf (accessed January 22, 2012).

—. *Public Papers of the Presidents of the United States: Dwight D. Eisenhower, 1957.* Washington, D.C.: U.S. Government Printing Office, 1958.

—. *Quadrennial Defense Review Report.* Washington, D.C.: Government Printing Office, September 2001.

—. *The National Military Strategy of the United States of America* Washington, D.C.: Government Printing Office, February 2011)

U.S. Government. *United States Northern Command.* October 1, 2002.
http://www.northcom.mil/ (accessed October 3, 2002).

U.S. President. *National Security Strategy.* Washington, D.C.: Government Printing
Office, May 2010.

—. *National Security Strategy.* Washington, D.C.: Government Printing Office,
September 2002.

—. *The National Strategy for Homeland Security.* Washington, D.C.: Government
Printing Office, July 2002.

U.S. War Department. *Annual Report of the Secretary of War, 1894.* Washington, D.C.:
Government Printing Office, 1895.

United States v. Red Feather, 392 F.Supp. 916 (D.C.S.D. 1975). April 7, 1975.
http://www.icdc.com/~paulwolf/cointelpro/law/USvRedFeather392FSupp916.htm
(accessed November 26, 2011).

United States v. Jaramillo. 380 F.Supp.1375 (D.C.S.D. 1974). August 14, 1974.
http://174.123.24.242/leagle/xmlResult.aspx?xmldoc=19741755380FSupp1375_1
1575.xml&docbase=CSLWAR1-1950-1985 (accessed November 30, 2011).

United States v. McArthur. 419 F.Supp. 186 (D.C.S.D. 1976). June 23, 1976.
http://174.123.24.242/leagle/xmlResult.aspx?xmldoc=1976605419FSupp186_156
2.xml&docbase=CSLWAR1-1950-1985 (accessed November 30, 2011).

Urwin, Gregory J. W. *The Army of the Constitution: The Historical Context.* Carlisle
Barracks, PA: Strategic Studies Institute, 2000.

Visco, E. P. "More Than You Ever Wanted To Know About Posse Comitatus." *United
American Freedom Foundation News.* November 16, 2005.
http://www.uaff.info/visco.pdf (accessed August 31, 2011).

Walker, David M. *Oxford Companion to Law.* New York: Oxford: Claredon Press, 1980.

Warner, John. *letter to Secretary of Defense Donald Rumsfeld.* 11 October 2001.

Weber, James R. "The Posse Comitatus Act of 1878: An Historical Perspective and
Implications for Homeland Defense." April 7, 2003.
http://www.dtic.mil/dtic/tr/fulltext/u2/a420136.pdf (accessed February 12, 2012).

West Virginia Division of Culture and History. *John Brown and the Harpers Ferry Raid.*
October 16, 1859. http://www.wvculture.org/history/jnobrown.html (accessed
October 29, 2011).

Young, Stephen. "Features - The Posse Comitatus Act: A Resource Guide." *LLRX.* February 17, 2003. http://www.llrx.com/features/posse.htm (accessed October 9, 2011).

www.ingramcontent.com/pod-product-compliance
Lightning Source LLC
Chambersburg PA
CBHW080529290526
45790CB00006B/2350